Falling
into
Enchantment

FALLING
INTO
ENCHANTMENT

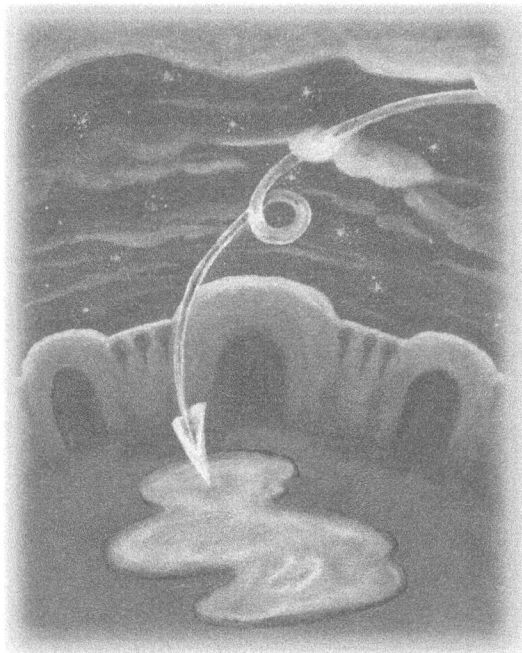

Poems from the 1970s in Santa Fe, New Mexico

Eleanor Grogg Stewart

SUNSTONE
PRESS

SANTA FE

Sunstone books may be purchased for educational, business, or sales promotional use.
For information please write: Special Markets Department, Sunstone Press,
P.O. Box 2321, Santa Fe, New Mexico 87504-2321.

Cover artwork by Reyes Padilla
Book and cover design › Vicki Ahl
Body typeface › Adobe Garamond Pro
Printed on acid-free paper
∞
eBook 978-1-61139-312-5

Library of Congress Cataloging-in-Publication Data

Stewart, Eleanor Grogg.
  [Poems. Selections]
  Falling into Enchantment : poems from the 1970s in Santa Fe, New Mexico / by
Eleanor Grogg Stewart.
    pages cm
  ISBN 978-1-63293-020-0 (softcover : alk. paper)
  I. Title.
  PS3619.T49377A6 2014
  811'.6--dc23
                            2014027112

WWW.SUNSTONEPRESS.COM
SUNSTONE PRESS / POST OFFICE BOX 2321 / SANTA FE, NM 87504-2321 /USA
(505) 988-4418 / ORDERS ONLY (800) 243-5644 / FAX (505) 988-1025

TO ALL THE BEAUTIFUL YOUNG MEN

CONTENTS

INTRODUCTION

The year was 1970. I arrived in Santa Fe at the Greyhound bus station on Water Street, and fell in love at first sight. A lot of people do; that's why New Mexico is called "The Land of Enchantment." I visited the director of a documentary film school on Canyon Road for a few days. Back in New York City where I was a somewhat-successful actress, I felt the overcrowded concrete city bearing down on me. I didn't want to do the rounds any more. I longed for that sunlit small strange city.

So, being young and fancy-free, I said goodbye to people and moved, taking only my clothes and a little cat called Chocolate Mouse whom I'd saved from a garbage heap. I thought I was hiding him in my room at La Fonda, the classic old hotel on the Plaza, but no doubt they knew he was there. In just a week, I located a small adobe-style house on a dirt road called *Camino Militar*. It was seventy-five dollars a month!

Chocolate Mouse went wild with joy chasing butterflies when I let him go outside. After I learned to light the fire in my fireplace and realized that I could sleep on the flat roof among the piñon trees if I put a mattress up there and discovered the hidden arroyo down the hill from my little magic house, I went wild with joy myself. It was the perfect place to write and to make love. That summer, I made a poet friend who asked me to ranch-sit for her near Cerrillos for a couple of weeks, although I had never been on a ranch and had no idea where Cerrillos was.

These poems are the story of my experiences in the Land of Enchantment during that 1970s period of newly found freedom and easygoing pleasures, but also of my immersion in other worlds among the people of the northern pueblos, the Din'e, the Lakota and the Apache—an experience that changed me forever.

Finally, I met someone whose Hispanic family had lived there since Santa Fe became a city in 1610, and we left New Mexico to travel. He returned to New Mexico after only one year, and eventually so did I—but only after many years of adventure in other worlds. But that's another story.

1

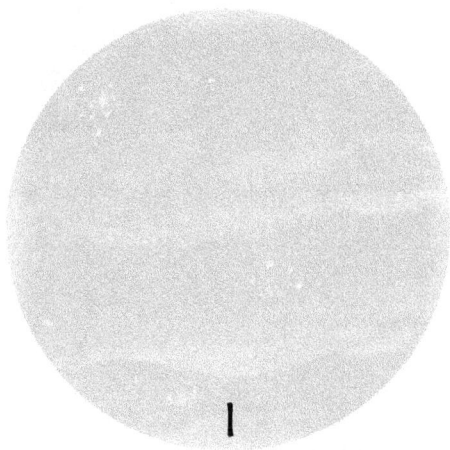

SUMMER AND CERRILLOS

Quick Sketch

A tall tough cowboy squinting in the sun
      one blue eye habitually closed, but watching me also from one eye

Then the invitation to coffee
      I introduce myself and he knows I'm not from here by my eyes

He puts "cowboy coffee" on to boil "full of cow dung and other bad things
      have to beat it back into the cup with a spoon"

He turns to me and finds my New York theater past
      and suddenly a revelation

In his rodeo days he'd followed a troupe—on the road I guess he meant
      from town to town

"They taught me how to live but it's been three years now
      and you lose it"

"They would take a midnight swim and they could make you see a leaf
      like you'd never seen it before"

Appreciation of actors, those who live in the now
      the artists of the first time

Not in Chicanos or in the hip but in a 45-year-old cowboy
      living on a hidden desert ranch

Frosty—a good cowboy name—"Are you one of them oddballs
      sensitive I mean?"

"Yes," I said. "Aren't you? Doesn't anyone ever hurt your feelings?"
      "Nope," he says and now he's back on cue

"Never let 'em get that close" and he goes out to his sweating buckskin
      seventeen hands high and hard to handle

The cows are sold; only four remain, but he's moving with the times
    he's training jockeys for the track

Girl jockeys, and he's proudly flashing back
    the hate he gets

For being a bachelor there with girls, "Them Texans is worried
    about their dirty little daughters"

Does he ever lose his iron control or not?
    too bad he has to need it

Driving Near Cerrillos

little animals that cross the road
on this rainy day
running rabbit
hopping toad
porcupine and pussycat
dragonfly and moth
brown cow black cow chewing slowly on
for stinkbugs I'm a small event
something to stand on their heads about
for others I am nothing
or I am their unexpected death
I love you small ones
and I will pass you safely if I can
if I am fast enough and wise enough
and do not dream too long

A Certain Sunset Near Cerrillos

none of your brilliant colors here
pale peach washes pale yellow
almost white behind the hills
which are every shade of blue
misty soft when distant
hard blue black nearby
brittle enough to break in pieces
wanting more than sight alone
touch or taste to know them
then unexpectedly at dark
a lume of tangerine across the sky
shakes my certainty
of the ending of this day
I shall love the sunset
let it lead me to the night
to probe it is to kill it
to follow it is life

Ranch Sitting Near Cerrillos

The horse kicked off the top of the fence
    the gerbil got locked in his cage
        the cat has shit where he shouldn't
            and the generator makes me rage

The windmill won't turn
    and the lamps won't burn
        and the kerosene's stinging my hands

The dog's disappeared
    just as I feared
        and the horses are all out of hay

I'm just past the fright
    alone here at night
        of futilely locking all locks

But your car's okay there
    with some minor repair
        and I'm awfully glad you're home home home
            it's good to see you home

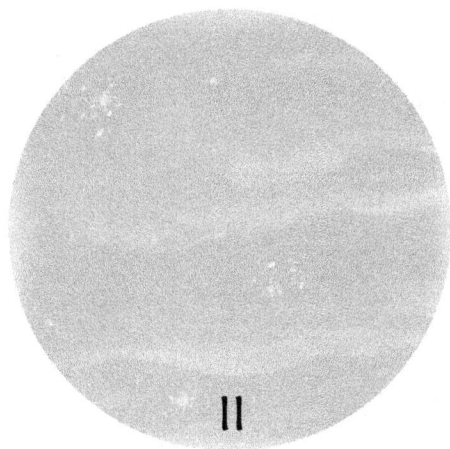

II

LAND OF MANY COLORS

On the Road to Taos

New Mexican hills
      bruised by the thumbprints of a passing cloud
      mesa'd, mauvely scattered green and brown
      more ancient, more desolate and dry
      than the hills of home

Yet there's unexpected
      lime green freshness of a single tree
      tender, tufted silver green of sage
      the charcoal brown of rocks
      and in my dry arroyo bed

Before a summer rainstorm
      drowned them in their night-time sleep
      red-orange, sunshine, violet
      I found a dozen kinds
      of brilliant, tiny weeds

On *Camino Militar*

my joy at these mountains
mammary mountains of Santa Fe
through my kitchen window
Dos Titos tip the sky
and now I see I'm standing
on a greenly bellied woman
my little house her womb

Thank God my world has changed
from sick cement and stone
and that I have arrived
before all the gentle ones are gone

Santo Domingo Man

TO TOUCH

        that feathered wave of blue black hair

TO HOLD

        abundant softly thick and full

AGAINST MY FACE

        scented musky sweet and strong

TO HAVE

        mystery returned—at last—returned for mine

Flamenco Dancer

if ovals of obsidian were lit from within

by their own black fire

and centered with

a laser beam of negative light

they would approach

the luster of Vicente's eyes

Miguel Angel

because you were the first I knew
because you touched my mind
because there is an unforgotten portrait
that sired a young girl's dream

Michael-angel

    apricot evening sky
    the dusty road I walk down
    people lounging in La Fonda
    and a motorcycle's roar

Michael

    the length of Canyon Road
    green ruana in the wind
    the sound of Spanish music
    and a double-rainbowed sky

Angel

    my crackling pinon fire
    the look of ancient wood

Devil

    an icy taste of hashish
    your hand between my thighs

Ordinary man

    because you were the first I knew
    because you touched my mind

Canyon Road Bar

Indian black hair flying
      pseudo hip and natural cool

Black man in gut deep pelvic jerk
      Anglo frontiersman seeking his rebirth

Long haired white chick
      half easy grace and half a wriggle

Melded by drink and leveled by rock
      a little blind in garish light

      Claude's of Santa Fe

Corn Dance

puuuure bluuuue sky
with skeins of cloud
and jet tracks
little bumpy clouds
like children's toys

BRINGER OF PEACE TO FILL MY NEED
BRINGER OF STORMS TO MATCH MY HEART

may I feel your autumn winds
and learn to trust the sun-surrounding rainbow ring
glowing its brief and special promise to
the belled shelled and feathered DANCERS
the sweating strong and lovely DANCERS
those painted fat and funny DANCERS
the enduring grave and dusty DANCERS
these ever evering evergeen DANCERS

who have danced all day
who have danced all day
to bring the corn

In the Sunlight There Are Rainbows in Your Hair

the walls of his room are lined with ghosts
the dead heroes of their dead indian past
technology has shown them how to glow
fluorescent pink and blue
ultraviolet lights the pupils of his eyes
until they are those of an animal
caught in the headlights of a car
or else a vampire in a film
and all our disembodied teeth
laugh and chatter in the dark
now they are superb young men
carelessly passing the night
now dormitory boys
cursing their devil the school
now young indians
haunted by their lives

Indians Are in this Year

"What did you think of it?" I'm asked of rodeo and corn dance
And I try to speak my truth though I may not please my hearer
Because I know that my truth changes, that experience is slow
That heat and dust are very rough on soft white woman flesh
That simplicity is earned and not often understood

It is like the tourist and one who comes to live
Both are strangers and naïve and both will make mistakes
Both would touch and try and both of course are white
One sees surfaces and the other looks for depths
One relates as "I and it" and the other tries for "I and Thou"

"You ask a lot" he says, "of us and of yourself
You stare too hard and try too hard to understand"
"The pressure of time", I say "But it's only your own time"
He'd seen a sensual verse I wrote, glorying in a man's black Indian hair
And then he stabbed me with a phrase, "Indians are in this year"

How can I tell him that I feel a kinship with these men
They have the artist's soul, they love beauty and they dance
They see behind words and respect the heart that speaks
They are mysterious but if there is a mystery it is in this
"I would be as simple as an ice cube melting in a glass"

III

BEAUTIFUL MEN

"Something About the Mist at Sunset and About Thinking"

for Simon

and he laughed when i came
soaking him with my juices
seeping into the sand
what do you want
tell me what you want
what could I want but this
to fuck in starlight
after firelight dies
to see your black hair
spreading on the sand
your spirit strong enough
to laugh and grip again
till the first cock crows
and we part to our own beds
and friends and lives and sleep

Randolfo Francisco Castillo

Randolfo Francisco Castillo
     as beautiful as fire
     as natural as earth
"The drums are the devil," he says
     and he attacks to conquer them
     to beat his will into them
Until even his magnetic power and energy
     must surrender to them
     and he comes back to this world
     on which he walks so lightly now
Clothed in his naked beauty
     and his long black hair
     wearing his virility
     like a color
     like a scent
And how they hate him for it
     I have seen it in their eyes
     for his youth and freedom
     which they gave up
     and never now can have
They would like to trap him
     cage him
     jail him
But he is too fleet for them
     his mind is virile too
     and I think
Randolfo Francisco Castillo
     if he doesn't scald his brain with drugs
     I think
This boy who wears his father's wedding jacket
     the twenty-five year-old bits of rice
     still lovingly left in the pockets
I think
     that he will get away

Who Is José

I brushed your shining hair and twined it in with mine
      a little slippery braid that slid apart
      as easily as we have done
                      Wake up José
      from your high school motorcycle dream
      and learn to own your name
                      Chicano
      why do you flinch at the word
      it is in the clean-boned beauty
      of your half-Indian face
      it is in the way you speak
      and in your glowing eyes
                      José you think
      is an old man's name
      a Spanish name
      and you are
      a young rock n' roar motorcycle dude
      flippin' wheelies and singin' Jethro Tull
      easy-walkin' with young kids
      who keep you as their brother-child

    You are José
    "I am Joaquin"
    You have become a man

The Hitchhiker

a hitchhiker in a buckskin jacket in the lightly falling rain
eleven stops he'd made on his journey into life
and when he stopped with me
it was with courtesy and fatigue
something held us bodily apart
although we shared a bed
and pieces of our lives
it was a little hard for him
not to pity me
and hard for me to take him
as solemnly as he did himself
but we found a meeting ground I think
I never can be sure
he didn't want for me to be like the other ten
he wanted me protected by a cloud of chastity
still he had moments of doubt about his choice
and then I teased him for revenge with a sexual poem
just to let him get a glimpse of what he'd missed

Jimmy

Young eyes turning watery and translucent from drink
      and sleepless nights
Imitation New York voice hip deep in telegraphic conversation
      powerful body its power unused
As warriors fell to decay in self-destructive anger once

The manuscript from his mind
      scattered – tender – funny – camp – and sane
Young community of determined laughter on the outside
      trying to get in
Bedbugs really do bite
      Sluggo in a velvet cap
Your tough guy role is played too well
      and Spanish dudes will cut your guts

The American dream has eaten your heart
      and is starting on your liver now
So Wisconsin boy – go home
      draw greening from your roots
Before you dare this world again

The Artist

outside are wind-driven snow
coinlike floating golden leaves
on the Rio Grande
and a wildness of horses

inside the ordinary things of life
and the usual pain of love
and a man I'd like to get to know
with his lion's mane of chestnut hair
his drawl and changing eyes
their brown intensity and go-by laughter
a western-hatted man
an artist and a master
of metal, wood and steel

kindle the cold winter
with a steady burning fire
I need your strong and
skillful hand against my mind

The Frog Prince

Once there was a handsome young prince
He was everything a prince should be
He was gentle and proud
He had long shining hair
His quiet voice made people stop their talk
To hear what he would say
His crown was red and white
He made everyone reveal a little of themselves
He belonged to no one

One day a woman came along and saw the prince
"How beautiful he is!"
She knew that she alone appreciated him
She alone saw into his eyes
And having a chariot nearby
She invited him for a ride
To her castle in the clouds
Floating together on the air
They shared a virgin kiss
And he turned into a frog
And then he hopped away

To the New Tom Paine

in the forests of new york city I found a bear
after three years of wolverines
a wonderful red bear
one of your old-time bears
your frontier bear
adventuring around the world
and recording it
in intricate bear's tracks
not for everyone to read
but he's a new bear too
lumbering in the burning woods
stamping on the fires to put them out
growling in his fury at neanderthal men
who ring the woods and don't care about its burning
who can only spend their time tormenting bears
until at last he whirls
a burning branch between his teeth
and charging hurls it back

I don't want to kill again you said
you've destroyed one universe
if you're god
create one now

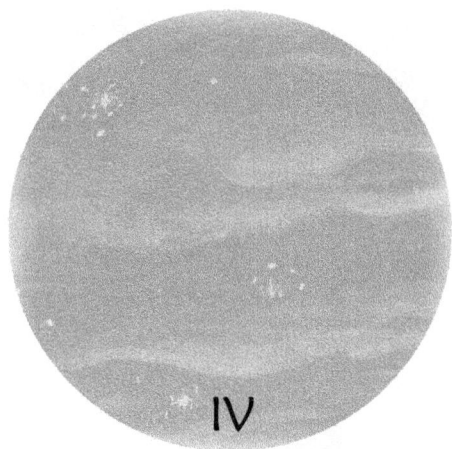

IV

THE DIN'E

Harry

today i think of you my friend
of your songs and trust
of stories from your life
and paintings in the sand
of the friendship bridge we've built
and walk on gingerly

A boy's memory of lights from oil wells in the night
While beauty songs were sung in his father's house
Of being sent to school where Navajo was never heard
Of hunger in the hogan while corn was being ground
Sweet coffee for a child to still the hunger pangs
And now a proud young man walks crying from a room
Where an indebted "friend" who'd taken tales from him
To publish in a book for money and for fame
Treats him like a child over one ten-dollar loan
And questions him like hired help
If he's going to return to a valued three-year job
And doesn't see the reason that he cries
Harry turns it down but gives no reason why
"Let him think" he says "and learn to understand"

Larry Casuse

He was too human to be spared
        the young Navajo
        with revolutionary eyes
        the only way I knew him
        was from a photo
        behind his student's glasses
        uplifted head
        youthful softness still plumped his cheeks

They say he killed himself
        but if he did
        it must have been
        that he was trapped
        and already hurt
        from ten minutes
        of concentrated fire
        into the store he held in Gallup
        what did he want to do?
        not to kill the Mayor
        or he would have
        he had the chance
        pulled the trigger twice
        on an uncocked gun
        to take some action
        he must have felt there was no other way

Now a crazy Indian's gone
        who'd managed to survive for nineteen years
        never to grow into his manhood
        never to go down to alcohol or drugs
        not to be more than a name
        known by a few for a few weeks
        except to the Din'e
        the People
        the Human Beings of this land

Gallup Ceremonial—1971

Young women rode with red paint on their cheeks
        and a banner crying "OUR LONG WALK MUST END"
While "Out of Order" signs closed off the restroom doors
        and the Big Chief Theatre had on "The Hallelujah Trail"
One slow drum beat its chilling sound
        passing down the lonely crowded street
Gallup—where the Indians sell from the backs of trucks
        and 50 cents gets you in to see the Anglo traders' goods
Gallup—where the cops smirk over cracks they make
        about Indian drunks—and it always rains
"Indian Capitol of the World"—when will you see
        that you who are the cause now blame what you have made
When you say they need your hock shops and your bars
        you are the one who's primitive and poor and boring in the end
For you flatten into sameness everything you touch
        and you'd need another fifty years to clean your streets of blood

***

Now I turn away and dream of what it might be like
if the Indian people ran this Indian feast

Land free for camping on which we'd be their guests
to pitch a family tent

Round dancing in the traffic-empty streets
"Out of Order" signs on Anglo merchants' doors

No more hot dog, burger, watery lemonade
but chile, deer meat, buffalo and fresh-made bread

To be shared together friendly in brush shelter or in tent
in tipi or in hogan around an open fire

Paper money to be banned and only trading to exist
a healing chance to learn another way of life

***

Could there then be laughter in the streets—the rules of an ugly world
        suspended for a while and we to dance the night?
For if you've ever danced to Indian drums, something lost will be returned
        and though you've only danced one time, you will remember and will yearn

V

JOURNEY TO OTHER WORLDS

APACHE WORLD

Buffy's Own Song
Mescalero, July 4, 1971

i carried water and carried it and carried it
you see that tree by itself
on the saddle of the mountain
i carried water to it every day
i sat over there
i never wore a jacket
just a blanket
and i sang my own songs
ey ah ey ah i ah ey
that's why i'm never afraid of the dark

my father planted that when i was born
you see it's in a line with the house
and then in a line with our mountain
now it's bigger than me
or maybe it's not as big
the moon glows through it
the sun glows through it
you see how it's always alone
its brothers and sisters are over there
that's why i'm always alone
the sky watered it
the stream watered it
my tears watered it
if i should die the tree would die too
maybe someday somebody will chop it down

the moon glows through it
the sun glows through it
i glow through it
if another tree would grow there by it
i might be with somebody too

let's go

Prayer For a Young Apache

THAT	the sins of our fathers not drag him down to alcohol death
THAT	our money lusts not break his pride
THAT	he walk between two worlds to the heartbeat drums
TILL	powdered braids hang below his waist

listen Darkness
to Che-gul-helch
thy namesake son
protect him
that
he not lose
his beauty
and his grace
please tonight
teach him
the courage of self control
and save him
from the bloody knife
the fear
the hunt
the prison cell
he is shy and laughing
he loves and he can give
let him go
Darkness
let him live

"I Never Said I Loved You But I Do"

in the light of dawn
i see your face
in our canvas tent
framed in a sleeping bag
and in your tangled hair
it glows copper
your smooth warm skin
that you should think it dark
worry about sunburn
fear that sulfur water might darken it
and yet Darkness is your name

> darkness did not protect you
> you could not make it to the trees
> the rocks where you could hide
> they caught you in a house
> put you against a wall
> and you fought for your life
> and this time kept it
> but they have killed your face
> with the ragged edges of a bottle
> and who will you be now my young friend
> and where will you find your pride

so long as we trusted ourselves
they could not touch us
one moment of doubt
and our fortress was down
but for a little while
outside of reason
there was a fragile love
goodbye now to your scarred young face
goodbye to your wind and honey-scented skin
to your stubborn tender proud
and haunted Mountain Spirit

One time after many weeks, he came back from that other world to give this gift to me, "I never said I loved you but I do. I love you. I will speak no more."

LAKOTA WORLD

Brulé Sioux

The Lakota are the People
Sioux we called them
enemy
brown slender enemy hands
young enemy
alone in Santa Fe
Navajo—Apache
Brule Sioux

Here in Santa Fe the earth itself requites
and the men who never lost the earth
who are not ashamed of making jewelry
with their hands
and who still will trust will gently trust
New York will never change them
hurt them, yes, rape their lives,
but will not now not ever
will not ever turn them white

my cloud-haired sioux-feathered love
wearing necklaces of turquoise
and the claws of hawks
a knife strapped onto belted jeans
knife scar on one shoulder two inches long
sometimes loving gentle
loving laughing passion
by firelight in white sand
slowly lovingly to build the fire
feed the living fire
sing—touch earth
blowing in me breath of love
moving in me lovingly
his cock his breath
and I come and come again
and flood his groin
and pour onto his belly

rivers oceans hotsprings of onflowing love
and he says to me
never be jealous
for my hand
is always on you
and he whispers
this is my love for you
as he arches from the bed
and lifts me up
thrusting to reach
the hotspring source
before he enemy
moans to his own height
murmuring in guttural Sioux voice
run baby run i am at your side
young enemy love
young Sioux
young tortured life
my enemy hand
white loving hand
is always
where oh where again
am always
there where
three worlds meet

Back to the belly of the serpent
coiled snake magnetic lines of force
dangerous spirit journey to another world
where my own soul returns to me
it had only gone a little way
I can dance it home
but only my own dance
not corn dance, deer dance, sun dance
but eleanor dance
white spirit dance
love dance

Lakota means countrymen
Snake we said
Sioux we said
Enemy

Dark Streets

dark streets
dark house
dark canyon
dark sky
dark heart
dark man

silvery black of melancholy
purple black of grief
half to black of empty pain
greenish black of dying plants
blue and black of bruis'ed flesh
red and black of blood and death
black on black of mind's despair

dark streets
dark house
dark canyon
dark skin
dark hair
dark thoughts

of a broken young Indian man

"I have killed my brother and I have to die"

Young Eagle

A wounded eagle came to me
    young and with a broken wing
I gave him food and stroked his wings
    I wanted him to fly so that
    I might see his beauty
    and fly with him to mountaintops

Sometimes he breasted soft against me
    sometimes he flapped his wings and fell
    in desperate attempts to fly
Once he lay in dull-eyed apathy
    without the will to preen his shining head
And once he turned his savage claws on me
    to tear and wound the one
    who loved but also frightened him
Exhausted by the fierce confusion of his spirit
    I journeyed to another place
When I returned the dogs had bayed him
    and my young eagle had already flown
    wounded still and far from home
    alone and lost in delusionary dreams
And in my hand I only hold
    a single feather from his wing

          eeeee-ai—fly
          young eagle fly
          "sleep on the wind"
          I will watch the skies
          for your return
          and I will know
          if you should fly
          too near the sun
          and fall in flames

PUEBLO WORLD

A Dream of Shalako

A curving silver arrow arched toward Shalako and found a
turquoise for its home.

***

    and i dreamed that a young man smiled at me
    and his eyes were more gentle than any i have known
    and he was wrapped in brilliant color
    and in his youth and in his strength
    and the spirit of the dance was in his lips
    the distance of the sky around in his exploring kiss
    and for me the night passed in simplicity and peace
    and i was for that slow moment safe
    and in my dream i never left that discovered home
    nor did he leave my side

Now I have awakened and still I move in grace. My ringless finger
calls him here to dream again if that could be—if that can be—

    a woman with a man

      Pueblo and Apache
      Navajo or Sioux

    the only bridge there is to cross

      all the Indian men
      who walk a shadowed way
      and whose lives I've touched
      in mixed delight and pain

except that it may be there is no bridge
no world for us to walk in light and free
it's been too long we've called them
redskins…injuns…bucks
chief or cochise on the street
and if one of us should love
she'll reap the whirlwind with the rest

the chasm is below and
it is lined with walls of ice
one long line of men behind you
one of women who've been ahead of me

and i dreamed that a young man smiled at me

they are the spirits
of the living and the dead

and he was wrapped in brilliant color
and in his youth and strength
and the spirit of the dance was in his lips
the distance of the sky around us
in his exploring kiss

my sisters speak to me
shall i crawl this bridge alone
screaming in silence
to these phantom men
in their double world
spitted on the twisting two-edged knife
of an indian love

and in my dream i never left
nor did he leave my side

***

A silver arrow fell at Shalako and forever now a turquoise is its
home.

VI

FAREWELL TO ENCHANTMENT

Claude's Again

after the passionate summer
the funky fall in Claude's
no cops cruising Canyon Road
to see who's hanging in the door
lounging in the street
and one young man is gone too
one who drew fire
and was both the degradation
and the passionate free spirit
of Claude's for me
barefoot and soft-voiced
dancing rapt to the drums
every story is about you
my hopeless Indian love

Rancho Encantado
(A dude ranch outside Santa Fe)

up front nothing above a whisper
but in back curses and sullen eyes
elegance in the service of mediocrity
hairdo faces less vital
than the lost lives
of the furs they wear
rough cross stolen from a Penitente's grave
Taos drum for idle feet to wiggle on
their shells their feathers and their eyes

to steal what these have made
is to steal the spirit
from which the object came
not a superstition but a subtle bond
between the maker and the thing
what is our passion to possess
to be sure we own it all
I have seen the cross and heard the drum
I can keep their spirits in my mind

New A.I.M. Member

he breaks horses he told me
and i believed him
for when i knew him he broke a lot of things
i saw that his arms are thin-boned and slender as a girl's
he can be broken too

on Canyon Road two years had passed
yet he spoke to me as though there'd been no time between
told me of his life showed me his work
said the Indians never dug into Mother Earth
got all they needed from six inches of soil

then we smoked and i told him about a cold night in a hogan
when i had left because i could not stay
when he wouldn't take my sleeping bag
though he stole my key
he looked shyly at me and then we kissed and he rode me

with a blue scarf around his neck
feeling the rhythm of the waterbed and moving exactly with it
he was a boy - a man - a black-maned colt
a turquoise earring hung beside his face
one hour later behind dark glasses in a public room
he would not even speak my name

Bird of Paradise

little bird who sings to me at unexpected times

delighting me in stores and on the road

you think no one can hear

when you betray what is loving in yourself

what is honest and unguarded

the way you go will take you far

but it will not lead you home

hatred will not line your nest

nor anger keep you warm

Bitter Tears

darkly brooding Chippewa man
of lust and semi-violence
but also of secret pain
never to be given a name of your own
sculptor and teacher in rimless glasses
dancing with thumbs hooked in belt
drunk – without that no violence at all
"the keys to my car"
"I'll get them in a minute"
too much liquor
but the dancing was so fine

> bitter tears
> bitter grass

too late now—his mind is gone
and all he wants is the feeling of revenge
my bitter tears exchanged for theirs
I left before dawn in white-faced strain
dry-eyed in the dark gray night
so what now draws my thoughts to you
(tonight you stroked my hair
silently and once in a public room)
it is your lambent grace and knowing
that locked inside your bitterness
there could be a tender love

Now Let's Hear It Girls

and now let's hear it girls
for that gorgeous Indian man
with his long black hair almost to his waist
and we're so ready to believe
that he's beautiful in all the other ways
and different from the men we knew
the money hungry
status seeking
power tripping
men we left behind
so we let him take us—use us—put us down
and all the time we're waiting
for a man who isn't there
until at last we start to see
that he's never with an Indian girl
and suddenly we know why
he's not so beautiful to them
they see him what he is
a money hungry
status seeking
power tripping
charming long haired boy
who takes without love
and gives almost nothing back
shows his white girls like trophies from his belt
and hides his feeling even from himself

New Mexico—Now
1974

none of it seems strange now
neither romantic nor beautiful nor strange
how many times do i have to learn again
we are all the same
it is how much of ambition
matched with how much of love
how much that one can take
where another one begins to break
how long we remain childlike
      childish
      chilled by reality
how much we can retain
regain of what we lost
or never had but knew about
define me by what i do for money
how i get my love
how much i show my age
what degrees i hold
or where i've been
      or live now
what i have forgotten
      or can retain

how well i talk or read
or if i've been in jail
they all matter terribly
      and not at all

my blood is blood
mi corrazon
my i—the little i
the only i there is

VII

DEPARTURE

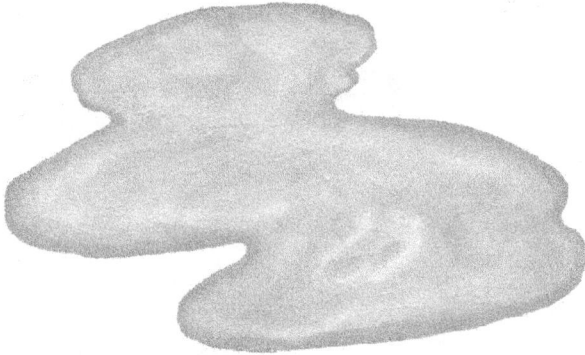

In the Moonth of Ashes Fire

in the moonth of ashes fire he went away
in the time when leaves open I will follow him

a man on horseback in the brilliant sun
the light he rides in is that I yearn for

       oh sunlit vision
       oh distant man
       the little mermaid
       from her ocean
       follows far behind

her singing tongue has been surrendered
her footprints blurred in blood

in the moonth of ashes fire he went away
in the time when leaves open I will follow him

The Little Mermaid by Hans Christian Anderson, was a tragedy. She gave up her immortality and her singing voice to become human. Her new feet bled where she walked. And the prince didn't fall in love with her. He married the princess he was supposed to marry. So the little mermaid climbed to the top of a cliff and threw herself into the ocean where she turned into green sea foam. It was my favorite fairy tale as a child, and I never knew why until I fell into enchantment in New Mexico.

ABOUT THE AUTHOR

This is Eleanor Grogg Stewart's first published poetry collection. Although she has written poetry for many years, she did not choose to publish for two reasons: first, she thinks that poetry is meant to be heard; and second, she was a teacher of college freshmen for forty-odd years and some of the poems did not seem appropriate for her students to read—perhaps an old-fashioned point of view.

Already published is a non-fiction work, *Not Only a Refugee*, the story of her time as a teacher for Vietnamese "boat people" in a UNHCR first asylum refugee camp on Palawan Island in the Philippines from 1982 to 1984. This was the most extraordinary experience of her life, and the book has helped her to reconnect with Vietnamese people who are now living full lives in many different countries.

Eleanor has a Bachelor's Degree from Marietta College in Ohio and a Master's Degree in theater from the University of Illinois. She was a professional actress for a number of years, performing mostly classical theater. Before she moved to New Mexico from New York City, she played Lady Capulet in Joseph Papp's production of "Romeo and Juliet" at the Theater in the Park with a young Martin Sheen as Romeo.

She has also taught public speaking and English composition to a variety of freshmen at Hunter College in New York City as well as educational institutions in Chicago, Denver, and New Mexico. In addition she taught English as a second language in Yokohama and Tokyo to a range of adult students including the first Japanese woman astronaut, Chiaki Mukai.

At the time of the publication of this book, Eleanor lives in Albuquerque, New Mexico, where she performs at poetry readings around the city.

9 781632 930200